Dear Kevin
Lead w/ haughter!
Dan

LEAVE A MARK, NOT A STAIN

LEAVE A MARK, NOT A STAIN

Leave a Mark, Not a Stain!

What every manager needs to know about using humor in the workplace

Patt Schwab. Ph.D.

LEAVE A MARK, NOT A STAIN

©2005 Patt Schwab

All rights reserved. No part of this publication may be reproduced, stored in a retrieval system or transmitted in any form or by any means electronic, mechanical, photocopying, recording or otherwise, without the prior written permission of the author.

Published by Rollingwood Press
9401 45th Ave NE
Seattle WA 98115

Printed in the United States of America

Cover Design by Warren Wilkins
Back cover design by Gretchen Flickinger
Editing and layout by Christine Dubois

ISBN: 1-59872-138-0

Order Information:

To order more copies of this book or to ask about other products and services offered by Dr. Patt Schwab, contact www.Fundamentallyspeaking.com

LEAVE A MARK

Humor, used well, is a mark of self-confidence, intelligence and an ability to connect effectively with others.

NOT A STAIN

Used incorrectly, it leaves a stain of ill will and incompetence that can take years to remove.

2 *LEAVE A MARK, NOT A STAIN*

CONNECT WITH HUMOR

This book is designed to promote "connective humor," the easiest and most effective form of workplace humor.

It is not the humor of sitcoms and stand-up performances. In fact, it's not really about joke telling as much as it is about finding and appreciating the lighter side of life and sharing that with others. Connective humor makes individuals feel they are part of a team and unleashes their creativity and loyalty.

My intent is to provide insight and ideas to enhance your use and understanding of humor as the critical management skill it is.

The examples in this book come from 30 years of practicing and observing humor in the workplace as a speaker, consultant, employee, and as a supervisor of staffs as large as 150 individuals. They range from my personal experiences to stories told by clients in Canada, Europe and the United States. They come from fields as diverse as health care, higher education, banking, forestry, private industry, association management, and federal, state, and local government.

Some of the following suggestions will be easy to implement from a supervisory position; others are probably more effective when put forward by selected staff members in collaboration with the leader. Some will fit your situation immediately; others will need to be adapted to your company culture. Some will make you chuckle; others may have you shaking your head in disbelief!

Just know that each idea worked somewhere, at some time. Since humor requires a measure of spontaneity, know, as well, that no one idea will work anywhere, forever.

Acknowledgements

Even little books like this one don't happen by themselves.

Thanks to all the clients, co-workers, staff and friends who shared their workplace humor and experiences with me over the years.

Thanks, especially, to those friends who shared (sometimes under the direct pressure of my pleading, sniveling and whining) their literary skills and insights: Edree Allen-Agbro, Evelyn Clark, Christine Dubois, Janet Luhrs, Dave Miller, Margy Peterson, Suzanne Price, Marilyn Schoeman-Dow, Bill Stainton, Nanne Wijma and Peggy Wolff.

6 LEAVE A MARK, NOT A STAIN

Dedication

To Mary and Dick Schwab, who taught me the power of connective humor, and showed me how, when mixed with love, it can create a marriage that after 62 years, is still going strong.

8 *LEAVE A MARK, NOT A STAIN*

Contents

Foreword: *Humor makes good cents* .... p. 15

Laughing Your Way to the Top! .... p. 17
    10 humor secrets strictly for managers

Managing to Connect with Humor .... p. 29
    30 humor hints to help your team,
    crew or staff get more smileage
    out of their workday

Smoothing Out the Rough Spots .... p. 49
    19 humor hints to help your staff
    reduce stress during difficult times

Meeting with Humor .... p. 65
    16 humor hints to enhance your
    meetings with humor

And in Closing. . . .. p. 77

Humor Hint Summary .... p. 79

10 *LEAVE A MARK, NOT A STAIN*

Foreword
Humor Makes Good Cents

A sense of humor is one of the top 10 traits of successful CEOs, and it's often listed as one of the top five leadership skills required for success. From mid-management levels on up, the primary criteria for advancement are interpersonal skills—specifically, communication skills with superiors, motivational skills with subordinates and rapport with clients.

Mark McCormick, author of *What They Don't Teach You in Harvard Business School*, says: "The most important asset in business is a sense of humor, an ability to laugh at yourself or the situation."

Headhunter firm, Robert Half International, and international temporary help firm, Accountemps, have done studies concluding that people judged as having a good sense of humor are frequently evaluated better on their work tasks as well as on their interpersonal skills. They are also rated as more creative, less rigid and more willing to consider new ideas and methods.

All other things being equal, the promotion will go to the person with the sense of humor.

Laughing Your Way to the Top

10 Humor Secrets Strictly for Managers

This book promotes "connective humor." That is to say, humor based on optimism and good will. We tend to trust people who make us laugh or smile. Laughter connects us at a visceral level and implies common experiences and values. We perceive such individuals as "safe" and feel more comfortable confiding in them.

As any manager knows, however, humor can also be used to belittle someone, undermine a situation or win an argument. While these humor practices seldom provide long-term workplace benefits or build a cohesive team, it is important to acknowledge and respect the dark side of humor's power.

The following executive summary identifies a few of the insights a leader gains by paying attention to the humor in his or her workplace.

1. There is humor in every workplace

If you don't see any humor in your office, it means that it has gone underground. And if you don't know about it, you are cut off from the pulse of the organization. Underground humor is often sarcastic, often directed at specific individuals or company values and seldom supportive of good service or high quality.

2. Humor is knowledge

If you know what people in your organization, facility or hospital are laughing at, you know what is going on. The kind of humor they use will tell you how healthy—or unhealthy—your organization is, and whether its real core values match those posted on the company website.

Are the jokes you hear positive or negative?

Are they about service or quality? Do they strike at unions, clients, competitors, patients or management? Are they about one department, division or project? Do they include people or exclude them?

In isolation, jokes don't mean much, but a rash of jokes on the same topic, from different sources, is worth attending to.

If the recurring topic is difficult customers, it could indicate that your customer service policy (or customer service reward system) needs tweaking. If the jokes are about another department or a staff group (physicians, nurses, faculty, sales, maintenance), it may mean that a personality conflict or a systemic issue is undermining communication, and, as a result, productivity. If they are about wasting time in meetings, it may be a clue that you need to upgrade your meeting skills.

3. Humor is not inherently good or bad—it's all in how it is used

We've all seen a well-timed humorous remark blow an idea, regardless of its merit, out of the water. We've also seen a similarly timed one ensure the acceptance of an idea—or at least extinguish debate on any competing proposals. That's a sample of the power that humor, wielded by an expert, can exert.

4. Humor can speed or slow change

Humor that is sexist, racist or homophobic, or humor that is against outside people or ideas, is usually designed to maintain the status quo. It reinforces stereotypes, limits thinking to gender- or ethnically-based roles, and makes staff afraid to take the risks that come with "thinking outside the box."

Humor that is supportive and inclusive invites change by helping to create an environment that encourages risk taking and the creative problem solving that accompanies it.

5. Some people have a hard time with humor

Excluding those who take offense at certain humor topics (racial, sexual, religious, etc.) or foul language (!@#$%^&*#@!, etc.), there are essentially three types of individuals for whom humor is a problem and one for whom jokes specifically are troublesome.

a. The person who was abused with humor as a child. These people were the butt of vindictive jokes or the object of sarcasm to the extent that they don't trust the joke-in-progress not to circle around and bite them. They need the security of a preface such as "A funny thing happened this morning. . ." or "I heard a cute joke. . ." before they can relax and enjoy the humor.

b. The individual who is burned-out with his or her job. These folks are so tired, bored or defeated that they cannot see the humor around them. Convinced that work is a painful chore, they reason that if people are laughing, by definition they are not working.

c. The person for whom control is very important. This is frequently a supervisor who feels a little uncertain about his or her skill level or his or her ability to cope with a situation. If control is your thing, then you intuitively know that it is more difficult to control laughing people than apathetic, scared or even moderately angry folks. This is why public figures would much rather have citizens angry at them than to have editorial cartoonists lampooning them.

d. Linear thinkers. Linear thinkers can have a wonderful sense of humor but tend to have difficulty with jokes. They are confused or annoyed when the punch line of a joke does not follow sequentially. A good joke setup leads the listener down one path and then surprises with a punch line flown in from an unexpected direction. Linear thinkers find this highly annoying–especially if the punch line comes at the end of a shaggy dog story to which they have committed five minutes listening time!

Since linear thinkers focus on logic, they often miss the connection between a joke's set-up and its punch line. For example, I use a one-liner that goes: "Don't give the project to him. He's so slow it takes him an hour-and-a-half just to watch *60 Minutes*." Generally in the United States, that line gets a laugh. In the logical thinking Netherlands, however, the response is usually, "How is that possible?"

6. Humor is a motivator

Companies are being told to be more productive, to be more accountable, to provide better customer service and enhanced quality control. And to do it all faster and cheaper.

In the 1990s, the average U.S. employee worked one month a year more than the average employee in the 1970s. And still, no one seems satisfied. What do you do?

My Ph.D. is in management, and I know there are essentially only three ways to motivate people to work harder, faster and smarter:

a. Threaten them. This is a dubious tactic in the best of times and doesn't work when your employees have other job opportunities. Needless to say, your best employees always have other job opportunities.

b. Pay them lots of money. This tactic is frequently more popular with the employees than with the stockholders. However, even if your company could afford to do it, Frederick Hertzberg's Motivation-Hygiene Theory showed decades ago that money is not a long-term motivator.

c. Make their work enjoyable. Create an atmosphere that is challenging, creative and fun.

Only the last one has been successful at effecting real change over time.

A humorous, positive atmosphere creates greater employee loyalty and increases productivity. Lest the image of your staff spending their days swapping jokes distract you, let me assure you that fun does not mean laughing all day. "Fun at work" means enjoying what you do, knowing you make a

difference, and feeling appreciated for your work.

7. Be careful about using sarcasm—especially when you're the boss

Sarcasm can be fun, no two ways about it!

The subtle put-down, the well-timed eye roll, the double entendre that, when directed at someone else, gives us an "in crowd" feeling—these can be addictive sensations.

The problem is that sarcasm creates an "us" verses "them" dynamic. It is always divisive. In the workplace, it can undermine morale and loyalty—an effect that is amplified when there is a power difference. Sarcastic remarks between boss and subordinate, physician and patient or clerk and customer, often carry far more weight than their initiator intended. Of all forms of humor, a sarcastic remark gone wrong is the most difficult to recover from.

I am not saying to ban sarcasm from your life entirely, I'm just urging you, as my friend Dr. Jean Wescott insists, to restrict sarcasm to interactions between "consenting adults."

8. Humor comes from the top

Researchers have found that with respect to creativity, which is closely related to humor, as much as 60 percent of the creativity in an organization comes from the boss.

This does not mean that the boss has to be the most creative (or the funniest) person in the organization. What this means is that you, as the boss, establish the penalty or reward for the risk-taking associated with humor and creativity.

9. Humor is usually initiated by the higher status person

An old maxim goes: If the joke you told wasn't funny, yet everyone laughed—you're the boss!

In a work environment, the boss' sense of humor (or lack thereof) is inevitably reflected by the staff. They not only laugh at the boss's jokes, but often try to tell similar ones to their own staff and colleagues.

Ideally, they laugh because the boss is genuinely funny. Be advised, however, that in some settings, they laugh because failing, or worse yet, refusing, to laugh at the boss's jokes can be seen as insubordination.

At the other end of the continuum, more than one boss has seen a subordinate's wise cracks in a meeting as a threat or leadership challenge. If the subordinate is a female or a younger male, the sense of threat often increases.

10. You don't need to be a clown to increase workplace humor

If you are in a leadership role, and don't see yourself as inordinately funny, an easy way to create laughter in your workplace is to support the humor of others around you.

Build a creative, positive workplace simply by providing a framework that encourages the playful, inventive, supportive side of your staff, colleagues, clients, customers or patients to emerge. Ask them to share their humor with you.

Laugh at their jokes. Leaven the action with a leading line like: "Tell me something funny that happened to you recently," or "Tell me about a success you had today." Allow them to create the humor, and then sit back and enjoy it with them.

Just remember, as the boss, the humor you respond to will be emulated by your staff. Be sure that you respond to humor that supports the goals you want to achieve.

Following are 65 easy-to-implement hints to help you develop, and maintain, a positive, productive and humorous workplace.

24   *LEAVE A MARK, NOT A STAIN*

Managing to Connect with Humor

30 Humor Hints to Help Your Team, Crew or Staff Group Get More Smileage Out of Their Work Day

If you want to create a team in a hurry, there are two things that will do it: a shared crisis or shared laughter. Laughter is cheaper—and a lot easier on your stress level.

Laughing together implies shared values and experiences. It builds stronger relationships with friends, associates and clients. As an added bonus, using humor well implies an ability to think creatively and to think on your feet.

Enough said. Do these things:

1. Take time to schmooze

Interacting with staff informally does not have to take a lot of time, and it can have a big payoff.

I am familiar with two cases where brilliant, but aloof, upper managers were told (one by his CEO, another by an organizational development consultant) that their effectiveness was hampered by an inability to establish rapport with their staff.

Their assignment, a great pre-emptive one for any manager, was to spend the first 15 minutes of the day visiting with the front line, talking to employees about anything except work. This meant asking questions about kids, spouse, sports—anything about which the employees were proud.

One individual told me that he had essentially been told, "Get friendly or get packing!" The assignment turned around his job and left him and his staff with a much better relationship. He continues spending "schmooze time" to this day.

2. Recycle Humor

Print up a series of jokes or one-liners on strips of paper, or gather up all those Joke-a-Day calendar pages and fold or crumple them up. Put them in a candy jar at the receptionist's desk or in the break room for people to take as needed for a low calorie pick-me-up. Note: they are also good medicine for folks with an Irony Deficiency!

3. Create a Fun Committee

Establish departmental or company-wide committees with the official job of keeping employees connected through laughter. Ask them to be responsible for one upbeat gag, stunt, or mini-show of appreciation each month or quarter. Give them a small budget to "play with." Some companies have made these committees secret, using the surprise factor to their advantage. Other groups, like the Ben and Jerry's Ice Cream Company "Joy Gang," go public so the staff can lobby them for specific events.

4. Use a humorous format for the company newsletter

An environmental engineering company designs each newsletter after a different popular magazine: *Business Weak, Readers Digress, Sly*, etc. It includes lots of informal articles and staff pictures as well as the standard fare about strategic planning, quality improvements and safety issues.

This is one of the few companies that can say that its newsletter not only gets read, it gets taken home and shared with employees' families!

5. Have a "Best Dressed Chicken" contest

Provide rubber chickens that staff can take home and dress using a chosen theme. Display the

chickens and let folks vote for their favorite. If you can only afford one chicken, do as one Washington state office did: Allow each interested staff member to check the chicken out for 24 hours, display it for one day, then post a photograph for the judging.

Plan ahead: September is National Chicken Month!

6. Invent "good fortune"

Print up a series of good fortunes, safety hints, or inside company jokes. Take them to a fortune cookie factory and ask them to insert them for you. NOTE: This is a surprisingly inexpensive way to add humor to an awards banquet or an employee appreciation day.

7. Encourage tacky tourism

Hold summertime contests to see who can bring back the best "tacky tourist" gift from his or her vacation. (My personal favorite was the tequila lollipop with a worm inside.) In addition to being a fun activity, this is also an inexpensive way to let clients or support staff know that you were thinking of them.

8. Check out the Teen Angels

Invite staff to bring in pictures of themselves as teenagers. (They are far more revealing than baby pictures!) Post the photos and have a contest to see who can recognize the most people.

9. Build a team while building caring citizens

If you want to build a strong team, make your team members feel proud of an accomplishment that is bigger than the workplace.

One state government office I worked with holds monthly luncheons to raise money for charity. Staff members donate the food and then pay a set fee to sample all the goodies. The lunches often feature cuisine from a particular ethnic or cultural group and include a bit of education about the group being celebrated. By Christmas, they have raised hundreds of dollars for shelters and other charities.

10. Baby, look at you now!

Establish a tradition where every time a baby is born to a member of your department, Mom and Dad are encouraged to bring the baby in and show it off. Having a baby around immediately humanizes the workplace. Take a picture of the whole team with the baby and then give the parent the rest of the day off.

11. Create positive events

Make a big deal over birthdays and special events. Hold potlucks, award ceremonies, ice cream feeds, dress down days—any activity that gives staff a chance to interact positively together. One construction company rotates a weekly BBQ through its work sites.

One year, to celebrate Secretary's/Support Staff Day, the managers I worked with rented a limousine, packed it with a picnic basket lunch and a bottle of champagne and sent our support staff on a three-hour city tour. (Three hours being the minimum time one could rent the limousine.)

Unfortunately, it did not cross our minds that our staff would buy additional champagne along the way. Their high-spirited return pretty much guaranteed not much work was accomplished the rest of the day! It did, however, make them grateful to us for years!

12. Celebrate staff successes

The Development Director at Steilacoom College walks around ringing a large bell to celebrate every time the school receives a gift or grant.

Physio-Control makes heart defibrillators and other life saving equipment. While employees take their work seriously, they don't take themselves seriously. One manager used to dress in a clown suit and ride a tricycle through the plant, throwing candy to the workers to celebrate reaching a production goal. "Spark Plug Awards" (real spark plugs encased in a Lucite block) are given to the work team members who most inspired, or "sparked," their group to work well together on a project.

13. Congratulate people

Employees at Washington State Department of Labor and Industries hold End-of-Project Celebrations when they finish a particularly large complicated project. All team members are included. Along with cake and small gifts, the celebration includes a recounting of "Tales of Bravery" over the life of the project.

When I asked one staffer what made her proudest about her job, her immediate answer was: "Seeing something you worked on posted on the wall during our Celebration of Accomplishments."

14. Post outlandish postcards

Souvenirs have increasingly become homogenous, with only the name of the town changing on the tee shirt, mug or baseball cap. Luckily, the lowly postcard still holds forth with a dash of regional flair.

Encourage your vacationing staff to send the silliest, most outlandish ones they can find back to the office. Post them on a bulletin board as laugh-inducing conversation starters.

15. Share good gossip

Make a daily habit of sharing at least three good things that happened to someone else on your staff or crew. It could be an award they received, or a funny story they told you, or the fact that they have beautiful flowers on their desk, or that their team won the softball game. Do this for a month and see what a difference it makes.

16. Incorporate jokes into meetings

One hospital administrative group starts each meeting by sharing a joke. The responsibility of coming up with the joke rotates through the attendees. The funniest moments often come from the dour individuals who deliver their material with the equivalent of "OK, here's my joke. Now let's get on with the meeting."

You can also use jokes to mark the change to a new topic during the meeting, or take a joke break in the middle of a long meeting.

17. Conduct a poster contest

There is a reason so many of the ads we see are funny: Funny is remembered.

What's the most effective sign (besides STOP) to make motorists use caution driving by road crews? "Give 'em a Brake!"

What is the best all time highway anti-litter sign? "Don't Mess with Texas!"

What does this mean for you? It means humorous posters just might sell your safety program or your new customer service initiative, or make one department understand the difficulty with which another one is struggling.

Don't leave the sloganeering to your marketing department. Remember that greatest of all management tenets: "People support what they help create."

Have a poster contest for the slogan *du jour* and let the marketing department gussy up the winner with the appropriate art work. It's an upbeat way to focus employees on company issues, and you might be surprised with what they come up with.

I challenged residence hall student staff to create something to cut down on weekend drinking. The winning poster was nothing an administrator would have come up with, but it was effective with the target population. It read:

> **VOMIT.**
> **Fall on your face.**
> **Act like a fool.**
> **Show everyone how much fun over-drinking can be.**

18. Establish an office joke board

Designate a bulletin board where staff, clients and/or patients can post humorous items. Encourage folks to bring in jokes and cartoons, perhaps by having a Humor Day when everyone brings in something for the board or by establishing a specific date, such as the first of each month, for staff to bring in new material.

After two weeks, remove the items and place them in a joke-book-in-progress (see #22). It is important to keep the jokes changing because it encourages staff to check the board and allows you to rotate negative humor out without seeming to censor it.

19. Give a prize for the best joke

This is a variation on the suggestion above and a particularly effective way to link staff working different shifts or in different facilities. Establish an office joke board and award a dollar a week for the best cartoon or joke submitted by a member of the staff.

Staff check in because they want to see which joke won—or to grouse that it wasn't the funniest. (Tell them it's your dollar, so you're making the decision!) Since jokes often reveal tensions, this is also a good way to check on staff morale.

20. E-mail/schleemail

Everyone knows e-mail is a quick and dirty way to get the word out. That's why it doesn't mean much to receive an e-mailed thank-you note.

If you are a supervisor who wants to make an impression, as well as model fantastic customer service, send individually hand written thank-you notes to your staff. Identify some specific contributions each individual made to help the team accomplish its task.

Many people are uncomfortable with public

recognition, but there are very few for whom a personal thank-you note from the boss will not elicit a sense of pride and a smile.

21. Toast new staff members

A man working for a nonprofit group shared a fun welcoming activity from his workplace with me. He said that his boss held a special staff meeting to toast new hires whenever they came on board. And toast was what she did! She brought in fancy jams and jellies, homemade bread, butter, and a toaster.

22. Create a "Share the Laugh" joke-book-in-progress

You know those great cartoons on your bulletin board—the ones that have turned yellow but you just can't toss them out? Here's a solution: Buy a photo album—the kind with plastic over each page—and put your jokes in it.

Keep this "Share the Laugh" joke-book-in-progress in your waiting room or at the reception desk for people to thumb through. It will give them a chuckle and make waiting more pleasurable.

If you have repeat clients or patients, encourage them to bring in jokes and cartoons to add to the collection. It builds a sense of loyalty and involvement with your business or clinic.

23. Expand your awards

Sure, give awards for the traditional accomplishments, but what's to stop you from awarding prizes for "Longest Commute," "Cleanest Cubicle," "Most Resilient," or anything else that strikes your fancy?

24. Host a candlelight breakfast

Celebrating a successful quarter or project completion with a candlelight dinner for your staff can not only cost a small fortune, but staff with carpools, childcare and countless other commitments may see it as an imposition, rather than as a show of appreciation.

Try, instead, a candlelight breakfast—ideally held during work time. It's novel, makes the same point, and is easier on the budget. Spice it up with some fun awards (Good Egg, Biggest Ham, Early Bird and the like) and toss in a novelty trinket as a reminder of the successful quarter or project.

The networking, good will and upsurge in production afterward will more than make up for the time "off work."

One Labor and Industries office added a powerful touch to the above. The supervisors individually hand wrote thank-you notes to each staff member, invited them to a candlelight breakfast and then served the meal. Talk about a morale boost!

25. Celebrate holidays that work for you

People are busy, distracted, even conflicted, over major holidays. When you need a real break or a celebration, look to obscure holidays. There is one darn near every day of the year begging to be noticed. Valuable opportunities such as Jan. 20, Penguin Awareness Day; March 18, Awkward Moments Day; April 25, Patt Schwab's Birthday

Day (alas, it is also Hairball Awareness Day); May 11, Eat What You Want Day; Aug. 8, Sneak a Zucchini Night; Oct. 18, Boost Your Brain Day; and even Shallow Person's Week, the second week in November; should not go uncelebrated!

One of the best days for a little workplace catharsis is Blame Somebody Else Day. This popular holiday is celebrated on the first Friday the 13th of every year.

NOTE: *The Obscure Holiday Handbook* has an extensive list of unusual, off-the-wall, but real holidays. Order information is in the back of this booklet or at www.FUNdamentallySpeaking.com.

26. Share not-so-funny things with humor

After staff at Highline College's Educational Planning & Advising Center discovered a typewriter had taken up desk space for five years while everyone thought someone else was using it, the manager, Gwen Spencer, decided it was time to clean house. A few days later, at her encouragement, the staff showed up for work dressed as a Merry Maid Brigade. Brandishing rags, cleansers, and dust mops, they proceeded to clean out the cabinets, update the bulletin boards, toss out old pamphlets, and, yes, get rid of the typewriter.

Adding the element of Merry Maid dress-up turned what could have been a tedious job into one that was fun, interactive and swiftly accomplished. As a bonus, it provided an easy team building experience and left the group with a collective memory of successfully and humorously solving a problem together.

27. Turn a negative into a positive

These days, companies frequently have staff working with colleagues or associates across the country—or world. Referrals are made, customers handed off, or telephone calls simply answered by whomever in a three-state time zone might be free. While the customer, at least ideally, does not notice these multi-mile transfers, the staff are often quite aware of them.

One of the smoothest tricks I have seen to connect such staff happened when a telephone company whose customer service division was in six states held an all-staff retreat. As retreat perks, staff were given disposable cameras and encouraged to photograph their counterparts from other states—the ones to whom they most frequently forwarded calls.

The cameras made for fun interaction at the retreat as individuals mugged for photos. Later, the photos, tacked up in cubicles, made for improved customer service. Staff glanced at them as they confidently handed customers off to an associate they now knew and liked.

28. Liven up Dress Down Day

Dress Down Day, or any repeated humorous activity, goes stale after a bit. Tweak the concept by focusing on one article of apparel. For example, hold a funny shoe or hat day. Pajama Days for nursing home staff can be a fun turn around for residents as well as employees.

29. Let your staff puzzle over award winners

The Washington Department of Retirement Services found a terrific way to start an all-staff retreat and simultaneously announce the recipients of the year's service awards. Photographs of the winners were blown up to 3 feet by 2 feet, glued onto poster board and then cut into large jigsaw puzzle pieces.

As staff arrived for the retreat, they were each given a puzzle piece and told to form groups based on who had the rest of that particular face. As they put the faces together, they found out who the award winners were.

When the event was over, the winners got to keep their jigsaw faces. Many of the puzzles later showed up on cubical walls with quizzical expressions as their owners moved the pieces around to express their feelings about a current project, meeting, or upcoming event.

30. Hire people who use humor as a problem-solving tool

A critical element in increasing a humorous atmosphere in your workplace is to hire funny people.

Years ago I called Nordstrom's training department to ask if they had a customer service program that could be exported to my staff at the

University of Washington. I was told that they didn't teach customer service.

"But you are famous for your customer service." I blurted out.

"True," was the reply, "but what we actually teach our sales associates is selling. We let their mothers teach them customer service!"

Of course they were right. It is far easier to hire caring employees with good interpersonal skills than it is to create them.

The fun SouthWest Airlines is famous for bringing to the more mundane aspects of flight travel, is not serendipitous. Southwest makes a concerted effort to hire staff with a caring, connective sense of humor. To do so, prospective employees are asked to give examples of how they used humor to defuse a difficult situation. It's a question that exposes the thought process and problem-solving skills of the interviewees, as well as their ability to use humor in tricky situations.

Smoothing Out the Rough Spots

17 Humor Hints to Help Your Staff Reduce Tension During Difficult Times

You are judged by the productivity of your staff, and a staff under too much stress is not productive. Reorganizations, new regulations, customers who are jerks—these are facts of life. So, unfortunately, is the emotional component that often accompanies them.

Your job is to help your staff navigate through difficult times as smoothly as possible. Taking a little time out for a humorous intervention often creates a huge pay-off in productivity.

Problems are resolved faster when the feelings behind them are acknowledged. The following techniques will help your employees deal with the emotional side of stress and free them to direct more of their problem-solving skills toward moving ahead.

1. Release tension with a Whine and Cheese party

Is the staff going through a tough period? Perhaps they are working on a tedious, time-consuming project, or the annual budget crisis has hit, or the noise from a major remodel next door is pounding its way through the walls. Call them together for a Whine and Cheese Party.  Pass around a plate of cheese and allow staff to whine cathartically, dramatically, about the problem.

A Whine and Cheese Party acknowledges their feelings, lets them know you understand, creates a sense of team (i.e. we're all in this together) and refocuses everyone on the issue at hand.

While struggling with a particularly arduous

project, my staff once scheduled weekly Whine and Cheese parties for the duration of the project. We added the caveat that no whining was allowed at any other time.

2. Burn votive candles

Lenore Donnenwirth, the Credit Manager of international candy company, Brown & Haley, leaves a lighted votive candle on her desk whenever she goes "upstairs" to negotiate her budget. This lets her staff know she is working for them. She likes to think their prayers, sent fervently in her direction, help her negotiate the best possible deal with the boss!

3. Play Pin the Blame on the ——

Outside individuals can create situations that sap your staff's energy and enthusiasm. Let your employees know that you understand, that you share their frustration, and, most importantly, that you have confidence they can rise above it.

A simple game of Pin the Blame on the Bad Guy (the corporate office, the competitor, the regulator, the Congress, or whomever) can often provide the necessary silliness, team building and tension relief to get the staff back to being productive.

Hang a flip-chart-sized drawing of the culprit on the wall, designate a spot where blame should be pinned and create your "blame" equivalent of the traditional Donkey tail. (Easy options for the latter are chunks of modeling clay; ink-smeared pieces of paper; coarsely torn, coffee-stained desk blotters, or, with the proper precautions, fat marker pens.)

Blindfold the affected individuals, provide them with a piece of blame, spin them around and let them have at it. Repeat until all affected parties had had their shot at it. Award a prize to the one who manages to apply the blame closest to the designated area.

4. Develop an office chant, song or whine for tough times

It works for sports teams, bands and major sales initiatives, why not for you and your staff? Tough times require more unity, and that's what a rallying cry can bring you. "We are in it together, we'll get through it together" is a powerful unifying force.

One office adapted the marching song from the Seven Dwarfs ("Hi Ho, Hi Ho, it's HOME from work we go!") They recorded it and played it (amplified throughout the building) at 5 p.m. every Friday to get themselves through a summer-long office renovation project.

5. Acknowledge the loss

Lost a major project or client? One famous reaction was that of an early Apple Computer staff group. After working on a software program for two years, the development team was told that top management had scrapped it.

To honor the depression everyone was feeling, the team took the diskettes with the rejected program, put them in a homemade coffin, rented a hearse and drove to a graveyard for a formal burial.

6. Create a Defenestration Resistance Award

The word "defenestration" means to throw someone or something out the window. A Defenestration Resistance Award would then be a customer service award given to the staff member who, although highly provoked, held his or her temper and resisted throwing someone (staff or customer) or something (a faulty computer, perhaps) out the window.

This is a particularly useful award for staff such as bank tellers, receptionists or nurses who have a lot of public contact. Provide a DR award for the person who handles the most difficult customer each week. Make it a good award: a bottle of champagne or permission to leave an hour early on a Friday. Watch how your staff begin to redefine the problem and actually LOOK for angry or upset customers to turn around!

7. Develop a "Laughter First Aid Kit" for the office

We know stress causes more than its fair share of accidents. Pre-empt it with an office "Laughter First Aid Kit." Solicit jokes, cartoons and riddles (singly or in books) from the staff. Above all, include props such as a moaning, groaning Tube of Gloom, a red nose, stress squeeze balls, finger puppets, a rubber chicken and anything else anyone cares to contribute. The Laughter Kit is also a great place to stash all the freebies you bring back from trade shows and conferences.

When staff members are frustrated, under the weather, or simply have the mubblefubbles, encourage them to check the Laughter First Aid Kit for something to help them get back on track.

8. Give your staff a breather

The Fred Meyer clerk checking me out had to confirm a price. She telephoned her manager, paused for a moment on the line and started laughing hysterically. I asked what was going on and she gave me the phone. All I could hear was a raspy breath barely hiding a chuckle. Still laughing, she said, "I've got the best manager in the world. I've been telling him all night I needed a breather, and now he's giving me one!"

9. Use a prop

When her city hall staff is having a difficult time with a project, Claire Gardner wears her Wizard of Oz "ruby slippers" to work. She frequently clicks her heels in an effort to take her staff home to Kansas.

To date, she says, they've not left Oregon (where they work), but her effort to get them to the peace and quiet of Dorothy's Kansas is appreciated. A bonus is that the Kansas relatives of two staff members have kept them supplied with tranquil postcards of Mennonite horse and buggies traversing the Kansas countryside.

10. Say a proper good-bye

Children's Hospital Home Nursing unit was moving from ratty old quarters by the hospital emergency room to a lovely new office suite in the administration building. The newly hired nurse manager, Joy Rogers, couldn't understand why her staff was dragging their feet over a move that seemed so advantageous. Gradually she realized that the staff, already distanced from the hospital by their work, was loath to give up a spot near the action-packed ER.

Since the move was a given, she suggested they say good-bye to their old quarters by recording all the significant events that had happened over the years in that location.

Furthermore, she suggested they do their recording on the walls! (Hey, the space was going to be torn down, why not?)

The staff had a wonderful time writing on the walls and remembering all the good (and bad) times they had shared there. When it came time for the move, they were ready. Besides, the place was so full of scribbles and graffiti, they were glad to go!

11. Hear the truth

The classified staff at Peninsula Community College have a choral staff group called the "Out To Lunch Bunch." They make their point in song parodies summarizing the year—and incidentally poke fun at the college administration, the Higher Education Board and even the Governor's Office if they feel so called.

For example, the college's active exchange program with Japan received a send-up when the lyrics of "Over the Rainbow" were changed to:

> *Somewhere over in Asia,*
> *My boss flies.*
> *If he flies over to Asia,*
> *Why, oh why, can't I?*

The group performs at the annual classified staff retreat and then, putting their jobs on the line, at the College President's management retreat. It's a modern version of the idea that the jester's role is to allow the king to hear the truth.

12. Designate an office scapegoat

Has your staff sunk into a negative mood? Is the desire to blame someone for every little thing that goes wrong sucking the energy and creativity out of them? The Fire Chief in an eastern Oregon town was fed up with the fault-finding culture of the City Hall staff. One day he brought in a beautifully hand-carved sign saying, "The person to blame for everything wrong this week is: _____!" He had carved a name plaque for every staff member. Each week a different person got to be "It." The City Clerk told me that the sign effectively ended the blame game by humorously illustrating how silly, ineffective and arbitrary it was to blame people.

13. Use a Roarin' Ryan Award to toast high-level goofs

The folks in the trenches know when upper management goofs. (Trust me on this!) If you want an open, creative organization, acknowledge the mistakes and move on. Put them into perspective with humor.

When he was promoted to Vice President for Business and Finance at the University of Washington, Jim Ryan's staff presented him with "The Roarin' Ryan Award." The award, a 4-ft. plywood cartoon of Ryan in a mail tunic guarding a bag of gold, became a focal point at the annual Christmas party.

It was awarded to the member of the university brass deemed to have made the most memorable goof that year. Recipients and runners-up, selected by the previous winner, were announced with fanfare and guffaws.

The award took on a life of its own, poking fun at deans, directors, vice presidents and faculty. In the process, it made the B&F Christmas party a campus event and connected the department with its campus clients.

The award had to be displayed prominently in

the recipient's office all year. When it was discovered that many winners were placing the award, face to the wall, behind their office doors, an artist was employed to paint the back of Knight Ryan onto the plywood. As an incentive to keep the award facing out, the back was painted with the chain mail drooping below Ryan's rump!

14. Tie up the loose ends

One year after major layoffs in a telecommunications company, the customer service staff held a retreat. They focused on humor, stress reduction, and mastering change in one's work and personal life.

The twist was that they invited the staff who had been laid off to attend the retreat.

It had been a tight work unit, and the layoffs were traumatic for the folks who stayed, as well as for those who had to leave. Staff who stayed felt guilty because close friends lost their jobs, frustrated because they had additional workloads, and unproductive because along with friends, they lost the network that kept them informed, expedited their work and connected them across departments.

In addition to giving the staff (laid off and retained) an opportunity to reconnect, the manager told me that she had two underlying agendas. She wanted the folks she had laid off to know that the layoffs were not personal and that they were missed—and remembered fondly. And she wanted the staff who had remained to see that most of their former colleagues were now happily established in new jobs.

It was one of the most powerful retreats I've ever attended. The manager was confident that the extra money spent to bring in her former staff was more than compensated by the renewed focus and commitment of the current staff.

15. Get more grades with honey

Getting faculty to turn in their grades before they left for summer was a chore for the Centralia College Registrar's office. The clerical staff recording the grades was in a one-down position to faculty members eager to take off for vacation.

Nagging, sulking, rolling eyes and mumbling under the breath hadn't worked, although all had been tried valiantly over the years. A switch to "honey" or in this case, homemade cookies, finally solved the problem.

Now, each fall, the Registrar's staff provides homemade cookies to all the faculty who got their grades in on time the previous spring. Amazing how it solved their late grade problem!

16. End a chapter gracefully

The weekend before the US West telephone company officially merged with Qwest, executives took the entire 700-person staff on a retreat.

They had presentations on stress, humor and goal setting. They recorded their US West history on butcher paper all over the walls of the retreat center. They ate, they drank, they played music and they remembered what for some were 25- to 30-year careers with the company. They said good-bye to US West.

Sunday they went home.

Monday they came to work ready to be fully a part of their new company.

17. Stop and smell the roses

When she spots one of her managers putting in too many late nights, one Alaska Airline Assistant Vice President sends the individual a dozen roses with a note to "stop and smell the roses."

The best meetings, like the best jokes, have good punch lines.

Meeting with Humor

16 Hints to Enhance Your Meetings with Humor

Adults learn best when they can interact. Individuals listening to a lecture about how to do a task retain less than those seeing someone do the task. When they actually do the task themselves, they learn the most.

So, too, the more involved participants at a meeting become and the more senses that are deployed, the better the information is retained. Laughter hooks information in at a visceral level that increases retention.

Two words of caution:

1. *Humor is not a gimmick, it is a powerful medium and deploying it for its own sake is seldom useful. The humor you encourage should support the purpose of your meeting, not distract from it.*

2. When intentionally introducing humor into a meeting that has not traditionally been known for its mirth, a small committee of staff members who are both funny and sensitive to the needs of others, will often be more successful than a single individual humorist.

1. Warm up with humor for greater creativity

A successful creative problem-solving session needs a warm-up to get staff in the free-thinking, risk-taking, oddball-connecting mindset necessary to incubate creative solutions. Starting a meeting with a few, fun, warm-up minutes solving Wacky Wordies or Droodles rewards the staff who come on time and helps stretch everyone's thinking.

Speaking of rewards, add some candy to your meetings. In addition to providing encouragement for staff to arrive on time, research shows that the playfulness of candy actually increases creativity.

2. Let Mr. Doggie do your whining and growling

Mr. Doggie was a hand puppet introduced at one of my staff meetings. His owner, Marsha, announced that if we put him on, we could growl or whine about anything we wanted "anonymously" and without retribution.

The collective look we gave Marsha said, "This is a professional staff group. That is a camp trick. Forget it!"

Finally, probably because he felt sorry for her, one of the staff put on Mr. Doggie, growled about something and passed him along. As Mr. Doggie worked his way around the table, complaints ranged from a recent root canal to items on the meeting agenda.

I became a believer when two of my staff actually growled and barked to resolution a petty complaint they had been squabbling over for weeks.

Mr. Doggie quickly became a mainstay at the staff meetings. Often he had nothing to say, but when he did, people listened!

ADDENDUM: I mentioned Mr. Doggie in a humor presentation to a group of foresters. A month later, one of the men called me and reported, "We thought Mr. Doggie was too wimpy for the US Forest Service."

I said that I understood, that my goal was simply to suggest lots of ideas, with the hope that one or more of them would fit a given group or personal style.

"No," he said, "You don't understand. We went out and bought 'Mr. Doberman!' "

3. Do I have to draw you a picture?

Sometimes the answer is "Yes!" At least it is if you want your staff in their "right" mind! Drawing often frees up the right hemisphere of the brain, which is the hemisphere that can sense the big picture—even when some of the puzzle pieces are missing.

Ask the attendees at your meeting to draw a picture of how they see the current problem or how they imagine the solution to the problem will look. Have them share their pictures and look for common threads, insights or new ideas.

It is important to stress that this exercise is best done by people with no artistic talent. The drawings work best when they hint at issues and need discussion to bring them out. For example, a squiggle indicating an argument works better than a drawing of two people in an angry discussion—and it's lots easier to draw!

For still another perspective, one staff group can be asked to free associate with a picture drawn by another group.

4. Create a meeting they will never forget

For an elaborate celebration at the end of a tough period or at the start of a major change, hire an outside group that specializes in just that sort of thing.

For example, when a large retailer seriously overbought inventory, Brian Walter's Extreme Meetings™ group brought in an Elvis impersonator to sing, "Return to Vender." Another time, during a Knights of the Roundtable spoof, a dragon (named after the competition) attacked during dinner. The executive team had to leap up and slay it in front of 700 laughing staff members.

(NOTE: For a program designed for your staff, you can reach Brian and Extreme Meetings at http://effectivenessinstitute.com.)

5. Emphasize that it's fowl to arrive late

One large Seattle consulting firm awards the office rubber chicken to the last person to arrive at the weekly staff meeting. That individual must then display the chicken in his or her cubicle and is charged with convening the meeting for the next week.

6. Make up skits or songs for difficult projects

This activity works best at a quarterly or division meeting as a way of celebrating the end of a difficult project or calendar year. Ask a few staff members or managers to do a skit for the group with a title such as: "The Worst or Best Day in the Life of . . . " (the clerical staff, the managers, the customers, the project itself).

It's a good staff tension reliever and an easy way for you to gain insight about the project.

7. "Pay the Pig" for negative talk

One Department of Transportation office acknowledged what we all know: There is a cost for cynicism, negative comments and the like. A giant piggy bank attends their meetings, and anyone who says something negative during the meeting has to "Pay the Pig." It has become such fun that they even charge people who are not at the meeting but who everyone "thinks" would have made a negative comment about a topic, had they been there!

At the end of the year, the money goes for a staff party. (Where, I assume, they pig out.)

8. Cool off a hot topic

Hot topic on the agenda? Hand out ice cream cones to chill folks out before beginning the discussion. It's difficult to be angry when you're eating a dripping ice cream cone!

9. Start with a Success Minute

Start your meeting by asking two to five members to take a minute to share something successful that happened to them recently. Keep the sharing under 10 minutes total or the task-focused members will get restless.

10. Share stories that reflect what you want

The owner of an asphalt paving company told me he once sent a crew to pave a tennis court. This is normally a four-hour job, and when the crew hadn't returned in almost eight hours, the boss took it upon himself to investigate. He quickly discovered that the tennis court was at a nudist camp!

He told me the crew insisted that the delay wasn't because the guys were gawking, but rather, it was the other way around: His grubby, rough paving crew was surrounded by naked sidewalk superintendents!

When he tells the story, the punch line is: "Unless your crew is working in a similar environment, I want your job finished on time!"

11. Share stories that show the inventiveness of your staff

In that same industry, asphalt pavement work crews are known to wrap a salmon or trout in tinfoil and let it cook on top of the paver engine all morning. Come lunchtime, they have a feast.

Stories abound about the supervisor who magically shows up at lunchtime "Just to see how the crew is getting along." Apparently such supervisors justify their behavior by sharing recipes among paving crews and projects.

12. Share Good News Minutes about folks who aren't there

Ask two to five members of your staff to share a success achieved by, or something good that happened to, a co-worker, a client, or another department.

This gives those at the meeting a positive connection to people and areas of the company they might not normally see. It's a quick and easy way to emphasize the larger organization and to reinforce a positive company vision.

13. Exploit the pizzazz of your presentation software

The phrase, "Oh great, another PowerPoint presentation" can be said with a positive lilt at the end, or with dripping sarcasm throughout. The latter reaction is most often associated with presentations featuring lots of small type on look-alike templates.

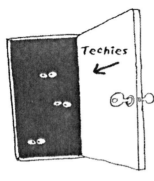

Lonely techies labored in the mines of Silicon Valley for years to develop computer-generated visuals that would let you draw on them, animate them, incorporate cartoons and photographs, circle important data and add appropriate sounds. Don't let their lives be wasted! Use the darn stuff.

Numbers on a consistently bland PowerPoint template should only be shown to insomniacs—and even then, not if they have to operate heavy equipment. If you want your audience to retain your information, use color and movement. Bright colors enliven even a dull topic, and movement instantly draws the eye.

Add cartoons and bright colors to your presentation materials. Use sound effects to make a point. Put a cartoon on the meeting agenda. If your computer has a good enough speaker, play an appropriate piece of music as the group convenes.

14. Show "Meetings, Bloody Meetings"

This timeless John Cleese training film, "Meetings, Bloody Meetings," is available at many public libraries. Cleese does a brutal dissection of how *not* to run a meeting and provides a springboard for a discussion about how much of the behavior in the film occurs at your meetings.

15. Let someone else get a laugh

Assign a different person each week to share a joke, cartoon or funny story. Start the meeting with the joke, or use the joke to mark the change to a new topic during the meeting. If you anticipate a long meeting, invite several folks to bring in material and take a joke break in the middle to re-energize the group.

16. Respond positively to humor as it presents itself

Remember, you are the boss. Your staff will notice what you respond to—whether it is with a smile, a guffaw or an air of reservation.

The humor that is most effective in meetings is not joke telling, but situational humor. This is the stuff that comes out of a shared insight, an unanticipated event, or a major blooper. Suddenly everyone is laughing so hard they are at risk of losing body fluids.

If you go home, tell the incident to a lukewarm audience, and conclude, "You had to be there," it was situational humor!

This is the kind of laughter that bonds groups together and establishes you as an insightful, witty leader.

And in closing . . .

Here are four statements that summarize what you need to know to use humor effectively in your workplace—or your life.

1. The best humor provides an affectionate insight into the situation.
2. Real humor comes from the heart— it's not a joke, it's a state of mind.
3. Behavior that gets rewarded, gets repeated.
4. People support what they help create.

74 *LEAVE A MARK, NOT A STAIN*

HUMOR HINT SUMMARY

30 Humor Hints to Help Your Team, Crew or Staff Group Get More Smileage Out of Their Work Day

1. Take time to schmooze
2. Recycle humor
3. Create a Fun Committee
4. Use a humorous format for the company newsletter
5. Have a "Best Dressed Chicken" contest
6. Invent "good fortune"
7. Encourage tacky tourism
8. Check out the Teen Angels
9. Build a team while building caring citizens
10. Baby, look at you now!

76 LEAVE A MARK, NOT A STAIN

11. Create positive events
12. Celebrate staff successes
13. Congratulate people
14. Post outlandish postcards
15. Share good gossip
16. Incorporate jokes into meetings
17. Conduct a poster contest
18. Establish an office joke board
19. Give a prize for the best joke
20. E-mail/schleemail

21. Toast new staff members
22. Create a "Share the Laugh" joke-book-in-progress
23. Expand your awards
24. Host a candlelight breakfast
25. Celebrate holidays that work for you
26. Share not-so-funny things with humor
27. Turn a negative into a positive
28. Liven up Dress Down Day
29. Let your staff puzzle over award winners
30. Hire people who use humor as a problem-solving tool

17 Humor Hints to Help Your Staff Reduce Stress During Difficult Times

1. Release tension with a Whine & Cheese Party
2. Burn votive candles
3. Play Pin the Blame on the _____
4. Develop an office chant, song or whine for tough times
5. Acknowledge the loss
6. Create a Defenestration Resistance Award
7. Develop a "Laughter First Aid Kit" for the office
8. Give your staff a breather
9. Use a prop
10. Say a proper good-bye

11. Hear the truth
12. Designate an office scapegoat
13. Use a Roarin' Ryan Award to toast high-level goofs
14. Tie up the loose ends
15. Get more grades with honey
16. End a chapter gracefully
17. Stop and smell the roses

16 Humor Hints to Add Vitality to Your Meetings

1. Warm up with humor for greater creativity
2. Let Mr. Doggie do your whining and growling
3. Do I have to draw you a picture?
4. Create a meeting they will never forget
5. Emphasize that it's fowl to arrive late
6. Make up skits or songs for difficult projects
7. "Pay the Pig" for negative talk
8. Cool off a hot topic
9. Start with a Success Minute

10. Share stories that reflect what you want
11. Share stories that show the inventiveness of your staff
12. Share Good News Minutes about folks who aren't there
13. Exploit the pizzazz of your presentation software
14. Show "Meetings, Bloody Meetings"
15. Let someone else get a laugh
16. Respond positively to humor as it presents itself

About the Author

Dr. Patt Schwab is owner of FUNdamentally Speaking, an international speaking and training company that believes in putting the "FUN" before "Da Mental!"

She shows midlevel managers and front-line staff how to use humor to increase rapport, resilience, and the bottom line.

Her programs are packed with laughter, insight, and practical tips for: managing people, coping with change, and enriching work and home life.

Patt combines years of hands-on management, teaching and training with work as a full time professional speaker in Europe, Canada and the USA. Her programs range from keynotes to full day seminars.

Dr. Schwab encourages her audience to look inside themselves for a humorous perspective on life's problems and challenges. She raises the philosophical question:

What if the Hokey Pokey IS What It's All About?

Patt holds academic degrees in History, Student Personnel, and Administration. Her doctoral thesis, on teambuilding, was titled, "People Support What They Help Create." She also holds the highest earned designation awarded by the National Speakers Association, the CSP, or Certified Speaking Professional.

Liven up your next meeting with a motivational humorist focused on helping you use humor to increase rapport, resilience, and the bottom line!

Some of Patt's popular presentations include:

Leave a Mark — Not a Stain!
(What every manager needs to know about humor in the workplace)

Creating a Legacy of Laughter
(Start investing in a legacy of fun)

When Hell Freezes Over—Ice S.K.A.T.E.!
(Mastering change and adversity)

S/He Who Laughs . . . Lasts!
(Humor as an interpersonal skill and workplace tool)

If You Don't Pause, Nothing Worthwhile Will Catch Up With You
(How to feel significant, competent and appreciated in a fast-paced world)

What If The Hokey Pokey IS What It's All About!
(Writing the next chapter of your life)

For a presentation tailored to your event and your organization, contact Patt in Seattle, Washington.

VOICE: 206-525-1031   **FAX: 206-525-8960**
E-mail: pattschwab@FUNdamentallySpeaking.com

Share your stories!

Let me know how you have applied the information in this book and/or tell me how you are using humor in your workplace.

There is a pocket-sized rubber chicken in it for you if you do!

E-mail your story to me at: Patt@FUNdamentallySpeaking.com

If you include some photos, I'll make sure they get posted on my website at:

www.FUNdamentallySpeaking.com

Where can I get a rubber chicken?

A Superior One—not one of those cheesy, fall-apart-with-the-first-womp-on-a-tabletop ones!

Funny you should ask!

If you want a quality rubber chicken (I was surprised too, there actually are quality differences between them), or a quality booklet on how to get more humor in your life at home or at work, fill out the form below and send it with the appropriate check (drawn on a solvent bank account) to:

Dr. Patt Schwab, 9401 45th Ave. NE, Seattle WA 98115

____Item _____ Quantity   Amount

Superior Rubber Chicken ($11) _____   _____
Rubber Chicken Key Chain ($2) _____   _____
Creating a Legacy of Laughter ($7.95) ___ _____
  60 Easy Ways to Add Humor to
  Your Daily Life
Humor Us: ($16.95)   _____   _____
  Fifteen of America's Funniest Humorists
  on the Power of Laughter
Leave a Mark, Not a Stain! ($14.95) ____ _____
  What Every Manager Needs to Know About
  Using Humor in the Workplace
Obscure Holiday Handbook ($10) _____   _____
Tax, Shipping & Handling included!   Total: _____

For a closer look at all our products, go to:
www.FUNdamentallySpeaking.com